IF JESUS WERE YOUR COUNSELLOR

IF JESUS WERE YOUR COUNSELLOR

COMPILED BY SELWYN HUGHES

"Steep yourself in God-reality, God-initiative, God-provisions. You'll find all your everyday human concerns will be met."

Luke 12:31-32

CWR Waverley Abbey House, Waverley Lane, Farnham,
Surrey GU9 8EP.

Selwyn would like to acknowledge the assistance of Ian Sewter in the preparation of this manuscript.

Concept development, editing, and production by CWR.
Design and typesetting by Simon Ray @ CWR Publishing.
Printed in Finland.
ISBN 1 85345 152 5
Cover photograph: Stone Images

For list of National Distributors see page 240.

CONTENTS

INTRODUCTION

On one occasion when I was in the United States, I came across a painting which depicted a businessman in a modern-day suit, sitting with a worried expression on his face before Jesus Christ, who was dressed in first-century garb. Christ's hand was outstretched and open as if making a point. It was clear from the painting that the artist meant to suggest that the businessman was being counselled by Christ.

For some time now the idea has lingered in my mind as to what Jesus would say to us if we brought to Him some of our modern-day questions. Would He say anything different from what He said to the men and women of His day? I think not.

In this book I have posed fifty questions for which there are clear answers given by Christ in the

Gospels. As a pastor and counsellor many of these questions have been asked of me at one time or another. But how much more powerful the answers are when one considers they are the actual words of the Master.

A few words of explanation, however, are necessary before you set out to use this book. In today's climate of counselling where counsellors are encouraged to be non-confrontational and non-judgmental, our Lord's answers might at first sound a little hard and lacking in compassion. Much of today's counselling is what is known as "client-centred". The counsellor avoids telling a person what to do but gently probes, asks key questions, reflects back, all with a view to helping the person come up with answers that seem right for them.

This is not Christ's way. He, above all other human beings, knows exactly what to say in answer to every question and that is why when He answers a question, you can be sure it is always the right answer. And everything He says is reality-based; Christ always tells it as it is.

I think, however, that our Lord's statements, although straight and to the point would come across with great compassion and love if He were sitting before you in the flesh. It is important to keep this in mind. His eyes, I believe, would show concern for you as a person and His tone of voice would be exceedingly tender, even when putting before you the strongest challenge.

He had nothing but contempt for hypocrites such as the Pharisees, but to anyone who is sincere and struggling, He says in effect: "I know you are hurting, I know you are struggling but I love you too much not to tell you it as it is." He is, after all, as the writer to the Hebrews put it: a high priest who is able to sympathise with our weaknesses (Hebrews 4:15). Once again I urge you to keep that firmly at the front of your mind as you read.

And if at times you are tempted to think He raises the standards to almost unbelievable heights, then remember also that He provides the strength by which we can reach up to them. All we have to do is provide the willingness to put into action what He advises; He supplies the power.

Another thing that needs to be remembered as you use this book is this: sometimes Christ's answers can be very obscure. You only have to peruse some of the stories Jesus told to be convinced of that. It is often thought that Jesus told stories to illustrate His meaning, but actually in many instances the opposite is true. Some of His stories reveal but most of them are intended to conceal.

I like what Eugene Peterson says about this: "Jesus' stories besides inviting us into a larger world than we presently inhabit pull us in as participants. These are not stories that entertain, that let us sit back and watch the action. More often than not one or another of them lodges unnoticed in our consciousness and then unexpectedly begins to release insights, to create new perspectives, to shift the very ground beneath us so that we find ourselves reeling, reaching out for wisdom."

The disciples once asked Jesus: "Why do you tell stories?" This was His reply: "You've been given insight into God's kingdom. You know how it works. Not everybody has this gift, this insight; …

Whenever someone has a ready heart for this, the insights and understandings flow freely. But if there is no readiness, any trace of receptivity soon disappears. That's why I tell stories: to create readiness, to nudge the people toward receptive insight. In their present state they can stare till doomsday and not see it, listen till they're blue in the face and not get it" (Matthew 13:10–13, *The Message*).

I imagine many people listened to Jesus' stories and went away shaking their heads wondering what it was all about. However, those who wanted to know would get the point. Understanding our Lord's stories is not a matter of IQ, but a desire to know the truth—even though the truth might hurt. When you approach the stories of Jesus from that standpoint then, believe me, the truth will come home to you.

On one occasion it is recorded that "All Jesus did that day was tell stories—a long storytelling afternoon" (Matthew 13:34, *The Message*). On still another occasion the high priests and leaders of the people came to Christ and demanded to see His credentials. "Who authorized you to teach here?" they asked. Jesus responded by saying; "First let me ask you a question. You answer my question and I'll answer yours. About the baptism of John—who authorized it: heaven or humans?" The high priests and leaders were on the spot because they knew if they said "heaven" Jesus would ask them why they did not believe in John's message. If they said "humans" they would be in trouble with the people because they all saw John as a prophet sent from God. They answered by saying "We don't know". Jesus then said, "Then neither will I answer your question" (Matthew 21:23–27, *The Message*).

My prayer is that as you read this book you will enter into the same experience as the two disconsolate disciples on the Emmaus Road who, as they reflected on what Christ said to them, remarked: "Were not our hearts burning within us while he talked with us on the road and opened the Scriptures to us?" (Luke 24:32, NIV).

I leave you now in the hands of Christ, the "Wonderful Counsellor" (Isaiah 9:6, NIV). Believe me, as someone who has counselled most of his life, and who knows many good and godly counsellors, they would not, I know, disagree with my final statement: you are in the best hands possible.

Selwyn Hughes

Issue 1

How can I make my Prayer Life more Effective?

"... Find a quiet, secluded place so you won't be tempted to role-play before God. Just be there as simply and honestly as you can manage. The focus will shift from you to God, and you will begin to sense his grace.

"The world is full of so-called prayer warriors who are prayer-ignorant. They're full of formulas and programs and advice, peddling techniques for getting what you want from God. Don't fall for that nonsense. This is your Father you are dealing with, and he knows better than you what you need. With a God like this loving you, you can pray very simply. Like this:

'Our Father in heaven,
Reveal who you are.
Set the world right;
Do what's best—as above, so below.
Keep us alive with three square meals.

Keep us forgiven with you and forgiving others.
Keep us safe from ourselves and the Devil.
You're in charge!
You can do anything you want!
You're ablaze in beauty!
Yes. Yes. Yes.'"[1]

"In prayer there is a connection between what God does and what you do. You can't get forgiveness from God, for instance, without also forgiving others. If you refuse to do your part, you cut yourself off from God's part."[2]

"Don't bargain with God. Be direct. Ask for what you need. This isn't a cat-and-mouse, hide-and-seek game we're in."[3]

"... When two of you get together on anything at all on earth and make a prayer of it, my Father in heaven goes into action. And when two or three of you are together because of me, you can be sure that I'll be there."[4]

"... That's why I urge you to pray for absolutely everything, ranging from small to large ... And when you assume the posture of prayer, remember that it's not all *asking*. If you have anything against someone, *forgive*—only then will your heavenly Father be inclined to also wipe your slate clean of sins."[5]

... "There was once a judge in some city who never gave God a thought and cared nothing for people. A widow in that city kept after him: 'My rights are being violated. Protect me!'

"He never gave her the time of day. But after this went on and on he said to himself, 'I care nothing what God thinks, even less what people think. But because this widow won't quit badgering me, I'd better do something and see that she gets justice—otherwise

I'm going to end up beaten black-and-blue by her pounding.'"

Then the Master said, "Do you hear what that judge, corrupt as he is, is saying? So what makes you think God won't step in and work justice for his chosen people, who continue to cry out for help? Won't he stick up for them? ..."[6]

"From now on, whatever you request along the lines of who I am and what I am doing, I'll do it. That's how the Father will be seen for who he is in the Son. I mean it. Whatever you request in this way, I'll do..."[7]

1.Matthew 6:6-13; 2.Matthew 6:14-15; 3.Matthew 7:7;

4.Matthew 18:19-20; 5.Mark 11:24-25; 6.Luke 18:1-7; 7.John 14:13

"I urge you to pray for absolutely everything, ranging from small to large."

Issue 2

When people hurt me, I find it hard to forgive

Let me tell you a story …

"The kingdom of God is like a king who decided to square accounts with his servants. As he got under way, one servant was brought before him who had run up a debt of a hundred thousand dollars. He couldn't pay up, so the king ordered the man, along with his wife, children, and goods, to be auctioned off at the slave market.

"The poor wretch threw himself at the king's feet and begged, 'Give me a chance and I'll pay it all back.' Touched by his plea, the king let him off, erasing the debt.

"The servant was no sooner out of the room when he came upon one of his fellow servants who owed him ten dollars. He seized him by the throat and demanded, 'Pay up. Now!'

"The poor wretch threw himself down and begged, 'Give me a chance and I'll pay it all back.'

But he wouldn't do it. He had him arrested and put in jail until the debt was paid. When the other servants saw this going on, they were outraged and brought a detailed report to the king.

"The king summoned the man and said, 'You evil servant! I forgave your entire debt when you begged me for mercy. Shouldn't you be compelled to be merciful to your fellow servant who asked for mercy?" The king was furious and put the screws to the man until he paid back his entire debt. And that's exactly what my Father in heaven is going to do to each one of you who doesn't forgive unconditionally anyone who asks for mercy."[1]

"This is how I want you to conduct yourself in these matters. If you enter your place of worship and, about to make an offering, you suddenly remember a grudge a friend has against you, abandon your offering, leave immediately, go to this friend and make things right. Then and only then, come back and work things out with God."[2]

"... Our Father is kind; you be kind.

Don't pick on people, jump on their failures, criticize their faults—unless, of course, you want the same treatment. Don't condemn those who are down; that hardness can boomerang. Be easy on people; you'll find life a lot easier. ..."[3]

"In prayer there is a connection between what God does and what you do. You can't get forgiveness from God, for instance, without also forgiving others. If you refuse to do your part, you cut yourself off from God's part."[4]

1.Matthew 18:23-35; 2.Matthew 5:23-24; 3.Luke 6:36-37;

4.Matthew 6:14-15

"Be easy on people;

you'll find life

a lot easier ..."

Issue 3

What is the Secret of Living under God's Blessing?

"You're blessed when you're at the end of your rope. With less of you there is more of God and his rule.

"You're blessed when you feel you've lost what is most dear to you. Only then can you be embraced by the One most dear to you.

"You're blessed when you're content with just who you are—no more, no less. That's the moment you find yourselves proud owners of everything that can't be bought.

"You're blessed when you've worked up a good appetite for God. He's food and drink in the best meal you'll ever eat.

"You're blessed when you care. At the moment of being 'care-full', you find yourselves cared for.

"You're blessed when you get your inside world—your mind and heart—put right. Then you can see God in the outside world.

"You're blessed when you can show people how to cooperate instead of compete or fight. That's when you discover who you really are, and your place in God's family.

"You're blessed when your commitment to God provokes persecution. The persecution drives you even deeper into God's kingdom.

"Not only that—count yourselves blessed every time people put you down or throw you out or speak lies about you to discredit me. What it means is that the truth is too close for comfort and they are uncomfortable. You can be glad when that happens—give a cheer, even!—for though they don't like it, *I* do! And all heaven applauds. And know that you are in good company. My prophets and witnesses have always gotten into this kind of trouble."[1]

1.Matthew 5:3-12

"You're blessed

when you're content

with just who you are

—no more, no less."

Issue 4

Is there a Point to my Being in This World?

"Let me tell you why you are here. You're here to be salt-seasoning that brings out the God-flavors of this earth. If you lose your saltiness, how will people taste godliness? You've lost your usefulness and will end up in the garbage."[1]

"Here's another way to put it: You're here to be light, bringing out the God-colors in the world. God is not a secret to be kept. We're going public with this, as public as a city on a hill. If I make you light-bearers, you don't think I'm going to hide you under a bucket, do you? I'm putting you on a light stand. Now that I've put you there on a hilltop, on a light stand—shine! Keep open house; be generous with your lives. By opening up to others, you'll prompt people to open up with God, this generous Father in heaven."[2]

"Let me give you a new command: Love one another. In the same way I loved you, you love one another. This is how everyone will recognize that you are my disciples—when they see the love you have for each other."[3]

"Here is a simple, rule-of-thumb guide for behavior: Ask yourself what you want people to do for you, then grab the initiative and do it for *them*. Add up God's Law and Prophets and this is what you get."[4]

1.Matthew 5:13; 2.Matthew 5:14-16; 3.John 13:34-35; 4.Matthew 7:12

"You're here to be

***salt-seasoning** that brings out*

the God-flavors

of this earth."

Issue 5

I worry about MONEY and MATERIAL things

"Don't hoard treasure down here where it gets eaten by moths and corroded by rust or—worse!—stolen by burglars. Stockpile treasure in heaven, where it's safe from moth and rust and burglars. It's obvious, isn't it? The place where your treasure is, is the place you will most want to be, and end up being. ...

"You can't worship two gods at once. Loving one god, you'll end up hating the other. Adoration of one feeds contempt for the other. You can't worship God and Money both.

"If you decide for God, living a life of God-worship, it follows that you don't fuss about what's on the table at mealtimes or whether the clothes in your closet are in fashion. There is far more to your life than the food you put in your stomach, more to your outer appearance than the clothes you hang on your body. Look at the birds, free and unfettered, not tied down to a job description, careless in the care of God. And you count far more to him than birds.

"Has anyone by fussing in front of the mirror ever gotten taller by so much as an inch? All this time and money wasted on fashion—do you think it makes that much difference? Instead of looking at the fashions, walk out into the fields and look at the wildflowers. They never primp or shop, but have you ever seen color and design quite like it? The ten best-dressed men and women in the country look shabby alongside them.

"If God gives such attention to the appearance of wildflowers—most of which are never even seen—don't you think he'll attend to you, take pride in you, do his best for you? What I'm trying to do here is to get you to relax, to not be so preoccupied with *getting*, so you can respond to God's *giving*. People who don't know God and the way he works fuss over these things, but you know both God and how he works. Steep your life in God-reality, God-initiative, God-provisions. Don't worry about missing out. You'll find all your everyday human concerns will be met.

"Give your entire attention to what God is doing right now, and don't get worked up about what may or may not happen tomorrow. God will help you deal with whatever hard things come up when the time comes."[1]

1.Matthew 6:19-34

"... you count

far more to him

than birds."

Issue 6

I am Afraid to Surrender to God's Will for my Life

... "Anyone who intends to come with me has to let me lead. You're not in the driver's seat; *I* am. Don't run from suffering; embrace it. Follow me and I'll show you how. Self-help is no help at all. Self-sacrifice is the way, my way, to saving yourself, your true self. What good would it do to get everything you want and lose you, the real you? What could you ever trade your soul for?"[1]

"If your hand or your foot gets in the way of God, chop it off and throw it away. You're better off maimed or lame and alive than the proud owners of two hands and two feet, godless in a furnace of eternal fire. And if your eye distracts you from God, pull it out and throw it away. You're better off one-eyed and alive than exercising your twenty-twenty vision from inside the fire of hell."[2]

"Do you want to stand out? Then step down. Be a servant. If you puff yourself up, you'll get the wind knocked out of you. But if you're content to simply be yourself, your life will count for plenty."[3]

"If you don't go all the way with me, through thick and thin, you don't deserve me. If your first concern is to look after yourself, you'll never find yourself. But if you forget about yourself and look to me, you'll find both yourself and me."[4]

"Don't be naïve. Some people will impugn your motives, others will smear your reputation—just because you believe in me. Don't be upset when they haul you before the civil authorities. Without knowing it, they've done you—and me—a favor, given you a platform for preaching the kingdom news! And don't worry about what you'll say or how you'll say it. The right words will be there; the Spirit of your Father will supply the words.

"When people realize it is the living God you are presenting and not some idol that makes them feel good, they are going to turn on you, even people in your own family. There is a great irony here: proclaiming so much love, experiencing so much hate! But don't quit. Don't cave in. It is all well worth it in the end. ..."[5]

1.Mark 8:34-37; 2.Matthew 18:8-9; 3.Matthew 23:11-12;

4.Matthew 10:38-39; 5.Matthew 10:17-22

"... If you forget about yourself and look to me, you'll find both yourself and me."

Issue 7

When someone has Hurt me What should I Do?

"If a fellow believer hurts you, go and tell him—work it out between the two of you. If he listens, you've made a friend. If he won't listen, take one or two others along so that the presence of witnesses will keep things honest, and try again. If he still won't listen, tell the church. If he won't listen to the church, you'll have to start over from scratch, confront him with the need for repentance, and offer again God's forgiving love."[1]

1.Matthew 18:15-17

"... confront him with the need for repentance, and offer again God's forgiving love."

Issue 8

When a person Becomes ONE of Your Followers late in life Does that MEAN He or She Has a Lesser Place in Heaven?

Listen to this story.

"God's kingdom is like an estate manager who went out early in the morning to hire workers for his vineyard. They agreed on a wage of a dollar a day, and went to work.

"Later, about nine o'clock, the manager saw some other men hanging around the town square unemployed. He told them to go to work in his vineyard and he would pay them a fair wage. They went.

"He did the same thing at noon, and again at three o'clock. At five o'clock he went back and found still others standing around. He said: 'Why are you standing around all day doing nothing?'

They said, 'Because no one hired us'.

"He told them to go to work in his vineyard.

When the day's work was over, the owner of the vineyard instructed his foreman, 'Call the workers in and pay them their wages. Start with the last hired and go on to the first'.

"Those hired at five o'clock came up and were each given a dollar. When those who were hired first saw that, they assumed they would get far more. But they got the same, each of them one dollar. Taking the dollar, they groused angrily to the manager, 'These last workers put in only one easy hour and you just made them equal to us, who slaved all day under a scorching sun.'

"He replied to the one speaking for the rest, 'Friend, I haven't been unfair. We agreed on the wage of a dollar, didn't we? So take it and go. I decided to give to the one who came last the same as you. Can't I do what I want with my own money? Are you going to get stingy because I am generous?'

"Here it is again, the Great Reversal: many of the first ending up last, and the last first."[1]

1.Matthew 20:1-16

"Here it is again, the Great Reversal: many of the first ending up last, and the last first."

Issue 9

What does it MEAN to be Successful from GOD'S Point of VIEW?

... "You've observed how godless rulers throw their weight around, how quickly a little power goes to their heads. It's not going to be that way with you. Whoever wants to be great must become a servant. Whoever wants to be first among you must be your slave. ..."[1]

"Don't look for shortcuts to God. The market is flooded with surefire, easygoing formulas for a successful life that can be practiced in your spare time. Don't fall for that stuff, even though crowds of people do. The way to life—to God!—is vigorous and requires total attention."[2]

1.Matthew 20:25-27; 2.Matthew 7:13-14

"The way to life—

to God!—

is vigorous and requires

total attention."

Issue 10

I know that One Day YOU will Return to this World in Power and Glory. When will that BE?

"But the exact day and hour? No one knows that, not even heaven's angels, not even the Son. Only the Father. So keep a sharp lookout, for you don't know the timetable ..."[1]

"God's kingdom is like ten young virgins who took oil lamps and went out to greet the bridegroom. Five were silly and five were smart. The silly virgins took lamps, but no extra oil. The smart virgins took jars of oil to feed their lamps. The bridegroom didn't show up when they expected him, and they all fell asleep.

"In the middle of the night someone yelled out, 'He's here! The bridegroom's here! Go out and greet him!'

"The ten virgins got up and got their lamps ready. The silly virgins said to the smart ones, 'Our lamps are going out; lend us some of your oil.'

"They answered, 'There might not be enough to go around; go buy your own.'

"They did, but while they were out buying oil, the bridegroom arrived. When everyone who was there to greet him had gone into the wedding feast, the door was locked.

"Much later, the other virgins, the silly ones, showed up and knocked on the door, saying, 'Master, we're here. Let us in.'

"He answered, 'Do I know you? I don't think I know you.'

"So stay alert. You have no idea when he might arrive."[2]

"... Be like house servants waiting for their master to come back from his honeymoon, awake and ready to open the door when he arrives and knocks. Lucky the servants whom the master finds on watch! He'll put on an apron, sit them at the table, and serve them a meal, sharing his wedding feast with them. It doesn't matter what time of the night he arrives; they're awake—and so blessed!"[3]

... "Watch out for doomsday deceivers. Many leaders are going to show up with forged identities claiming, 'I'm the One'. They will deceive a lot of people. When you hear of wars and rumored wars, keep your head and don't panic. This is routine history, and no sign of the end. Nation will fight nation and ruler fight ruler, over and over. ...

"Stay with it—that's what is required. Stay with it to the end. You won't be sorry; you'll be saved."[4]

"... I'm A to Z, the First and the Final, Beginning and Conclusion.

"How blessed are those who wash their robes! The Tree of Life is theirs for good, and they'll walk through the gates to the City."[5]

1.Mark 13:32; 2.Matthew 25:1-13; 3.Luke 12:36-38; 4.Mark 13:5-13b;

5.Revelation 22:13-14

"So stay alert.

You have no idea

when he might arrive."

Issue 11

I Know that as a Christian I am Called to a life of "Stewardship". What Does THIS Involve?

"There was once a man descended from a royal house who needed to make a long trip back to headquarters to get authorization for his rule and then return. But first he called ten servants together, gave them each a sum of money, and instructed them, 'Operate with this until I return.'

"But the citizens there hated him. So they sent a commission with a signed petition to oppose his rule: 'We don't want this man to rule us.'

"When he came back bringing the authorization of his rule, he called those ten servants to whom he had given the money to find out how they had done.

"The first said, 'Master, I doubled your money.'

"He said, 'Good servant! Great work! Because you've been trustworthy in this small job, I'm making you governor of ten towns.'

"The second said, 'Master, I made a fifty percent profit on your money.'

"He said, 'I'm putting you in charge of five towns.'

"The next servant said, 'Master, here's your money safe and sound. I kept it hidden in the cellar. To tell you the truth, I was a little afraid. I know you have high standards and hate sloppiness, and don't suffer fools gladly.'

"He said, 'You're right that I don't suffer fools gladly—and you've acted the fool! Why didn't you at least invest the money in securities so I would have gotten a little interest on it?'

"Then he said to those standing there, 'Take the money from him and give it to the servant who doubled my stake.'

"They said, 'But Master, he already has double . . .'

"He said, 'That's what I mean: Risk your life and get more than you ever dreamed of. Play it safe and end up holding the bag.

" 'As for these enemies of mine who petitioned against my rule, clear them out of here. I don't want to see their faces around here again.' "[1]

1.Luke 19:12-27

"Risk your life and get

more than you ever dreamed of.

Play it safe and end up

holding the bag."

Issue 12

How do I AVOID Spiritual Barrenness?

"Live in me. Make your home in me just as I do in you. In the same way that a branch can't bear grapes by itself but only by being joined to the vine, you can't bear fruit unless you are joined with me.

"I am the Vine, you are the branches. When you're joined with me and I with you, the relation intimate and organic, the harvest is sure to be abundant. Separated, you can't produce a thing. Anyone who separates from me is deadwood, gathered up and thrown on the bonfire. But if you make yourselves at home with me and my words are at home in you, you can be sure that whatever you ask will be listened to and acted upon. This is how my Father shows who he is—when you produce grapes, when you mature as my disciples.

"I've loved you the way my Father has loved me. Make yourselves at home in my love. If you keep my commands, you'll remain intimately at home in my love. That's what I've done—kept my Father's commands and made myself at home in his love.

"I've told you these things for a purpose: that my joy might be your joy, and your joy wholly mature. This is my command: Love one another the way I loved you. This is the very best way to love. Put your life on the line for your friends. You are my friends when you do the things I command you. I'm no longer calling you servants because servants don't understand what their master is thinking and planning. No, I've named you friends because I've let you in on everything I've heard from the Father.

"You didn't choose me, remember; I chose you, and put you in the world to bear fruit, fruit that won't spoil. As fruit bearers, whatever you ask the Father in relation to me, he gives you.

"But remember the root command: Love one another."[1]

1 John 15:4-17

"Make yourselves

at ***home*** *in*

my love."

Issue 13

Why is the World so Hostile to Your Followers?

"If you find the godless world is hating you, remember it got its start hating me. If you lived on the world's terms, the world would love you as one of its own. But since I picked you to live on God's terms and no longer on the world's terms, the world is going to hate you.

"When that happens, remember this: Servants don't get better treatment than their masters. If they beat on me, they will certainly beat on you. If they did what I told them, they will do what you tell them.

"They are going to do all these things to you because of the way they treated me, because they don't know the One who sent me. If I hadn't come and told them all this in plain language, it wouldn't be so bad. As it is, they have no excuse. Hate me, hate my Father—it's all the same. If I hadn't done what I have done among them, works no one has *ever* done, they wouldn't be to blame. But they saw the God-signs and hated anyway, both me and my Father. Interesting—they have verified the truth of their own Scriptures where it is written, 'They hated me for no good reason.'"[1]

1.John 15:18-25

"Servants don't get

better treatment

than their masters."

Issue 14

I often Hurt PEOPLE by my Careless WORDS. How can I Overcome this?

"... Let me tell you something: Every one of these careless words is going to come back to haunt you. There will be a time of Reckoning. Words are powerful; take them seriously. Words can be your salvation. Words can also be your damnation."[1]

"Don't pick on people, jump on their failures, criticise their faults—unless, of course, you want the same treatment. That critical spirit has a way of boomeranging. It's easy to see a smudge on your neighbor's face and be oblivious to the ugly sneer on your own. Do you have the nerve to say, 'Let me wash your face for you,' when your own face is distorted with contempt? It's this whole traveling road-show mentality all over again, playing a holier-than-thou part instead of just living your part. Wipe that ugly sneer off your own face, and you might be fit to offer a washcloth to your neighbor."[2]

"Don't pick on people, jump on their failures, criticize their faults—unless, of course, you want the same treatment. Don't condemn those who are down; that hardness can boomerang. Be easy on people; you'll find life a lot easier. ..."[3]

"You're familiar with the command to the ancients. 'Do not murder.' I'm telling you that anyone who is so much as angry with a brother or sister is guilty of murder. Carelessly call a brother 'idiot!' and you might just find yourself hauled into court. Thoughtlessly yell 'stupid!' at a sister and you are on the brink of hellfire. The simple moral fact is that words kill."[4]

1.Matthew 12:36-37; 2.Matthew 7:1-5; 3.Luke 6:37; 4.Matthew 5:21-23

"Words can be your salvation. Words can also be your damnation."

Issue 15

I Am Afraid to Die

"... I am, right now, Resurrection and Life. The one who believes in me, even though he or she dies, will live. And everyone who lives believing in me does not ultimately die at all. ..."[1]

... "First things first. Your business is life, not death. Follow me. Pursue life."[2]

"... I say this with absolute confidence. If you practice what I'm telling you, you'll never have to look death in the face."[3]

"It's urgent that you listen carefully to this: Anyone here who believes what I am saying right now and aligns himself with the Father, who has in fact put me in charge, has at this very moment the real, lasting life and is no longer condemned to be an outsider. This person has taken a giant step from the world of the dead to the world of the living.

"It's urgent that you get this right: The time has arrived—I mean right now!—when dead men and women will hear the voice of the Son of God and, hearing, will come alive. Just as the Father has life in himself, he has conferred on the Son life in himself. …

"... The time is coming when everyone dead and buried will hear his voice. Those who have lived the right way will walk out into a resurrection Life; those who have lived the wrong way, into a resurrection Judgment."[4]

"... Those who are included in the resurrection of the dead will no longer be concerned with marriage nor, of course, with death. They will have better things to think about, if you can believe it. All ecstasies and intimacies then will be with God. ..."[5]

1.John 11:25-26; 2.Matthew 8:22; 3.John 8:51; 4.John 5:24-29;

5.Luke 20:35-36

"And everyone who lives

believing in me

does not *ultimately*

die at all."

Issue 16

I Find it Hard to be Generous

"... Give away your life; you'll find life given back, but not merely given back—given back with bonus and blessing. Giving, not getting, is the way. Generosity begets generosity."[1]

"... Give a cool cup of water to someone who is thirsty, for instance. The smallest act of giving or receiving makes you a true apprentice. You won't lose out on a thing."[2]

"When he finally arrives, blazing in beauty and all his angels with him, the Son of Man will take his place on his glorious throne. Then all the nations will be arranged before him and he will sort the people out, much as a shepherd sorts out sheep and goats, putting sheep to his right and goats to his left.

"Then the King will say to those on his right, 'Enter, you who are blessed by my Father! Take what's coming to you in this kingdom. It's been ready for you since the world's foundation. And here's why:

I was hungry and you fed me,
I was thirsty and you gave me a drink,
I was homeless and you gave me a room,
I was shivering and you gave me clothes,
I was sick and you stopped to visit,
I was in prison and you came to me.'

"Then those 'sheep' are going to say, 'Master, what are you talking about? When did we ever see you hungry and feed you, thirsty and give you a drink? And when did we ever see you sick or in prison and come to you?' Then the King will say, 'I'm telling the solemn truth: Whenever you did one of these things to someone overlooked or ignored, that was me—you did it to me.'

"Then he will turn to the 'goats,' the ones on his left, and say, 'Get out, worthless goats! You're good for nothing but the fires of hell. And why?

Because—

I was hungry and you gave me no meal,
I was thirsty and you gave me no drink,
I was homeless and you gave me no bed,
I was shivering and you gave me no clothes,
Sick and in prison, and you never visited.'

"Then those 'goats' are going to say, 'Master, what are you talking about? When did we ever see you hungry or thirsty or homeless or shivering or sick or in prison and didn't help?'

"He will then answer them, 'I'm telling the solemn truth: whenever you failed to do one of these things to someone who was being overlooked or ignored, that was me—you failed to do it to me.' "[3]

1.Luke 6:38; 2.Matthew 10:42; 3.Matthew 25:34-45

"The **smallest act** of giving or receiving makes you a true apprentice."

Issue 17

I'm Confused by Those who Say There are Many Paths to God

... "I'll be explicit, then. I am the Gate for the sheep. All those others are up to no good—sheep stealers, every one of them. But the sheep didn't listen to them. I am the Gate. Anyone who goes through me will be cared for—will freely go in and out, and find pasture. A thief is only there to steal and kill and destroy. I came so they can have real and eternal life, more and better life than they ever dreamed of."[1]

... "I am the Road, also the Truth, also the Life. ..."[2]

"... Rivers of living water will brim and spill out of the depths of anyone who believes in me this way, just as the Scripture says."[3]

1.John 10:7-10; 2.John 14:6; 3.John 7:38

"I am the Road,

also the Truth,

also the Life."

Issue 18

I Worry about what Other People Think of Me

"There's trouble ahead when you live only for the approval of others, saying what flatters them, doing what indulges them. Popularity contests are not truth contests—look how many scoundrel preachers were approved by your ancestors! Your task is to be true, not popular."[1]

"Don't be bluffed into silence by the threats of bullies. There's nothing they can do to your soul, your core being. Save your fear for God, who holds your entire life—body and soul—in his hands."[2]

1.Luke 6:26; 2.Matthew 10:28

"Your task

is to be true,

not popular."

Issue 19

I Feel Deeply Insecure about the Future

"Give your entire attention to what God is doing right now, and don't get worked up about what may or may not happen tomorrow. God will help you deal with whatever hard things come up when the time comes."[1]

"... Don't be afraid of missing out. You're my dearest friends! The Father wants to give you the very kingdom itself."[2]

"... I'm leaving you well and whole. That's my parting gift to you. Peace. I don't leave you the way you're used to being left—feeling abandoned, bereft. So don't be upset. Don't be distraught."[3]

"... Look at the ravens, free and unfettered, not tied down to a job description, carefree in the care of God. And you count far more.

"Has anyone by fussing before the mirror ever gotten taller by so much as an inch? If fussing can't even do that, why fuss at all? Walk into the fields and look at the wildflowers. They don't fuss with their appearance—but have you ever seen color and design quite like it? The ten best-dressed men and women in the country look shabby alongside them. If God gives such attention to the wildflowers, most of them never even seen, don't you think he'll attend to you, take pride in you, do his best for you?"[4]

1.Matthew 6:34; 2.Luke 12:32; 3.John 14:27; 4.Luke 12:24-28

" The Father wants

to give you the

very kingdom itself."

Issue 20

You talked much about the "Kingdom of God". What really is the nature of this Kingdom?

"God's kingdom is like an estate manager who went out early in the morning to hire workers for his vineyard. They agreed on a wage of a dollar a day, and went to work.

"Later, about nine o'clock, the manager saw some other men hanging around the town square unemployed. He told them to go to work in his vineyard and he would pay them a fair wage. They went.

"He did the same thing at noon, and again at three o'clock. At five o'clock he went back and found still others standing around. He said, 'Why are you standing around all day doing nothing?'

"They said, 'Because no one hired us.'

"He told them to go to work in his vineyard.

"When the day's work was over, the owner of the vineyard instructed his foreman, 'Call the workers in and pay them their wages. Start with the last hired and go on to the first.'

"Those hired at five o'clock came up and were each given a dollar. When those who were hired first saw that, they assumed they would get far more. But they got the same, each of them one dollar. Taking the dollar, they groused angrily to the manager, 'These last workers put in only one easy hour, and you just made them equal to us, who slaved all day under a scorching sun.'

"He replied to the one speaking for the rest, 'Friend, I haven't been unfair. We agreed on the wage of a dollar, didn't we? So take it and go. I decided to give to the one who came last the same as you. Can't I do what I want with my own money? Are you going to get stingy because I am generous?'

"Here it is again, the Great Reversal: many of the first ending up last, and the last first."[1]

... "God's kingdom is like a farmer who planted good seed in his field. That night, while his hired men were asleep, his enemy sowed thistles all through the wheat and slipped away before dawn. When the first green shoots appeared and the grain began to form, the thistles showed up, too.

"The farmhands came to the farmer and said, 'Master, that was clean seed you planted, wasn't it? Where did these thistles come from?'

"He answered, 'Some enemy did this.'

"The farmhands asked, 'Should we weed out the thistles?'

'He said, 'No, if you weed the thistles, you'll pull up the wheat, too. Let them grow together until harvest time. Then I'll instruct the harvesters to pull up the thistles and tie them in bundles for the fire, then gather the wheat and put it in the barn.' "

... "God's kingdom is like a pine nut that a farmer plants. It is quite small as seeds go, but in the course of years it grows into a huge pine tree, and eagles build nests in it."

... "God's kingdom is like yeast that a woman works into the dough for dozens of loaves of barley bread—and waits while the dough rises."[2]

"God's kingdom is like a treasure hidden in a field for years and then accidently found by a trespasser. The finder is ecstatic—what a find!—and proceeds to sell everything he owns to raise money and buy that field."[3]

1.Matthew 20:1-16; 2.Matthew 13:24-33; 3.Matthew 13:44

"God's kingdom

is like yeast that a woman works

into the dough for bread—

and waits while the dough rises."

Issue 21

Lust and Sexual Desire Seem to Rule My Life

"You're blessed when you get your inside world—your mind and heart—put right. Then you can see God in the outside world."[1]

"… don't think you've preserved your virtue simply by staying out of bed. Your *heart* can be corrupted by lust even quicker than your *body*. Those leering looks you think nobody notices—they also corrupt.

"Let's not pretend this is easier than it really is. If you want to live a morally pure life, here's what you have to do: You have to blind your right eye the moment you catch it in a lustful leer. You have to choose to live one-eyed or else be dumped on a moral trash pile. …"[2]

"Using the legalities of divorce
as a cover for lust is adultery;
Using the legalities of marriage
as a cover for lust is adultery."[3]

1.Matthew 5:8; 2.Matthew 5:28-29; 3.Luke 16: 18

*"You're **blessed***

when you get your inside world

— your mind and heart—

put right."

ISSUE 22

I AM EASILY TEMPTED

"... Stay alert; be in prayer so you don't wander into temptation without even knowing you're in danger. There is a part of you that is eager, ready for anything in God. But there's another part that's as lazy as an old dog sleeping by the fire."[1]

"... stay on your toes. Satan has tried his best to separate all of you from me, like chaff from wheat. ... I've prayed for you in particular that you not give in or give out. When you have come through the time of testing, turn to your companions and give them a fresh start."[2]

1.Matthew 26:41; 2.Luke 22:31-32

"I've prayed for you

in particular that you

not give in

or give out."

Issue 23

What does it TAKE to BE A LEADER in Your Church?

"... Whoever wants to be great must become a servant. Whoever wants to be first among you must be your slave. That is what the Son of Man has done: He came to serve, not be served—and then to give away his life in exchange for the many who are held hostage."[1]

"Be wary of false preachers who smile a lot, dripping with practiced sincerity. Chances are they are out to rip you off some way or other. Don't be impressed with charisma; look for character. Who preachers *are* is the main thing, not what they say. A genuine leader will never exploit your emotions or your pocketbook. ..."[2]

"... You address me as 'Teacher' and 'Master,' and rightly so. That is what I am. So if I, the Master and Teacher, washed your feet, you must now wash each other's feet. I've laid down a pattern for you. What I've done, you do. I'm only pointing out the obvious. A servant is not ranked above his master; an employee doesn't give orders to the employer. If you understand what I'm telling you, act like it—and live a blessed life."[3]

1.Matthew 20:26-28; 2.Matthew 7:15-16; 3.John 13:13-17

"So if I, the Master

and Teacher, washed your feet,

you **must now**

wash each other's feet."

Issue 24

What is the Ultimate End of Those who Do NOT accept You as Saviour and Lord?

"... God didn't go to all the trouble of sending his Son merely to point an accusing finger, telling the world how bad it was. He came to help, to put the world right again. Anyone who trusts him is acquitted; anyone who refuses to trust him has long since been under the death sentence without knowing it. And why? Because of that person's failure to believe in the one-of-a-kind Son of God when introduced to him.

"This is the crisis we're in: God-light streamed into the world, but men and women everywhere ran for the darkness. They went for the darkness because they were not really interested in pleasing God. Everyone who makes a practice of doing evil, addicted to denial and illusion, hates God-light and won't come near it. ..."[1]

1.John 3:17-20

"He [God] came to help,

to put the world

right again."

Issue 25

I have Committed a Serious sin Can I be Forgiven?

"Listen to this carefully … There's nothing done or said that can't be forgiven. …"[1]

(To see how Jesus dealt with a person who had engaged in a serious sin, read the following.)

Jesus went across to Mount Olives, but he was soon back in the Temple again. Swarms of people came to him. He sat down and taught them.

The religion scholars and Pharisees led in a woman who had been caught in an act of adultery. They stood her in plain sight of everyone and said, "Teacher, this woman was caught red-handed in the act of adultery. Moses, in the Law, gives orders to stone such persons. What do you say?" They were trying to trap him into saying something incriminating so they could bring charges against him.

Jesus bent down and wrote with his finger in the dirt. They kept at him, badgering him. He straightened up and said, "The sinless one among you, go first: Throw the stone." Bending down again, he wrote some more in the dirt.

Hearing that, they walked away, one after another, beginning with the oldest. The woman was left alone. Jesus stood up and spoke to her. "Woman, where are they? Does no one condemn you?"

"No one, Master."

"Neither do I," said Jesus. "Go on your way. From now on, don't sin."[2]

1.Mark 3:28; 2.John 8:1-11

"There's nothing

done or said

that can't be forgiven."

Issue 26

I've Fallen out with someone; How do I put things Right?

"If a fellow believer hurts you, go and tell him—work it out between the two of you. If he listens, you've made a friend. If he won't listen, take one or two others along so that the presence of witnesses will keep things honest, and try again. If he still won't listen, tell the church. If he won't listen to the church, you'll have to start over from scratch, confront him with the need for repentance, and offer again God's forgiving love."[1]

"Here is a simple, rule-of-thumb guide for behavior. Ask yourself what you want people to do for you, then grab the initiative and do it for *them*. Add up God's Law and Prophets and this is what you get."[2]

"... If you enter your place of worship and, about to make an offering, you suddenly remember a grudge a friend has against you, abandon your offering, leave immediately, go to this friend and make things right. Then and only then, come back and work things out with God."[3]

1.Matthew 18:15-17; 2.Matthew 7:12; 3.Matthew 5:23-24

"Ask yourself what you want people to do for you, then grab the initiative and do it for them."

Issue 27

I am no Worse than Most people and Better than some

Let me tell you a story …

"Two men went up to the Temple to pray, one a Pharisee, the other a tax man. The Pharisee posed and prayed like this: 'Oh, God, I thank you that I am not like other people—robbers, crooks, adulterers, or, heaven forbid, like this tax man. I fast twice a week and tithe on all my income.'

"Meanwhile the tax man, slumped in the shadows, his face in his hands, not daring to look up, said, 'God, give mercy. Forgive me, a sinner.' "

... "This tax man, not the other, went home made right with God. If you walk around with your nose in the air, you're going to end up flat on your face, but if you're content to be simply yourself, you will become more than yourself."[1]

1.Luke 18:9-14

"God, give mercy.

Forgive me,

a sinner."

Issue 28

I Feel So terribly Lonely

"... I will talk to the Father, and he'll provide you another Friend so that you will always have someone with you. This Friend is the Spirit of Truth. The godless world can't take him in because it doesn't have eyes to see him, doesn't know what to look for. But you know him already because he has been staying with you, and will even be *in* you!

"I will not leave you orphaned. I'm coming back. In just a little while the world will no longer see me, but you're going to see me because I am alive and you're about to come alive. At that moment you will know absolutely that I'm in my Father, and you're in me, and I'm in you.

"The person who knows my commandments and keeps them, that's who loves me. And the person who loves me will be loved by my Father, and I will love him and make myself plain to him. ...

"... a loveless world ... is a sightless world. If anyone loves me, he will carefully keep my word and my Father will love him—we'll move right into the neighborhood! ..."[1]

"Look at me. I stand at the door. I knock. If you hear me call and open the door, I'll come right in and sit down to supper with you. ..."[2]

1.John 14:15-23; 2.Revelation 3:20

"If you hear me call

and open the door,

I'll come right in and

sit down to supper with you."

Issue 29

What can You Tell me about Heaven?

"... There is plenty of room for you in my Father's home. If that weren't so, would I have told you that I'm on my way to get a room ready for you? And if I'm on my way to get your room ready, I'll come back and get you so you can live where I live. ..."[1]

"Watch that you don't treat a single one of these childlike believers arrogantly. You realize, don't you, that their personal angels are constantly in touch with my Father in heaven?"[2]

1.John 14:1-3; 2.Matthew 18:10

"There is plenty

of room for you

in my Father's home."

Issue 30

I am PUT OFF by CHRISTIANS Who DON'T Live UP to Your STANDARDS

"... What's that to you? You—follow me."[1]

"Staying with it—that's what God requires. Stay with it to the end. You won't be sorry, and you'll be saved. ..."[2]

"Don't quit, even if it costs you your life. Stay there believing. I have a Life-Crown sized and ready for you."[3]

1.John 21:22; 2.Matthew 24:13; 3.Revelation 2:10

"Staying with it

—that's what

God requires."

Issue 31

What Should Be My Attitude to Money and Material Things?

"Don't hoard treasure down here where it gets eaten by moths and corroded by rust or—worse!—stolen by burglars. Stockpile treasure in heaven, where it's safe from moth and rust and burglars. It's obvious, isn't it? The place where your treasure is, is the place you will most want to be, and end up being.

"Your eyes are windows into your body. If you open your eyes wide in wonder and belief, your body fills up with light. If you live squinty-eyed in greed and distrust, your body is a dank cellar. If you pull the blinds on your windows, what a dark life you will have!

"You can't worship two gods at once. Loving one god, you'll end up hating the other. Adoration of one feeds contempt for the other. You can't worship God and Money both."[1]

"No worker can serve two bosses:
He'll either hate the first and love the second
Or adore the first and despise the second.
You can't serve both God and the Bank."[2]

1.Matthew 6:19-2; 2.Luke 16:36

"Don't hoard treasure down here

where it gets eaten by moths

and corroded by rust or—

worse!—stolen by burglars."

Issue 32

Others think I am a Good Christian but sometimes I Suspect my own Motives

"Be especially careful when you are trying to be good so that you don't make a performance out of it. It might be good theater, but the God who made you won't be applauding.

"When you do something for someone else, don't call attention to yourself. You've seen them in action, I'm sure—'playactors' I call them—treating prayer meeting and street corner alike as a stage, acting compassionate as long as someone is watching, playing to the crowds. They get applause, true, but that's all they get. When you help someone out, don't think about how it looks. Just do it—quietly and unobtrusively. That is the way your God, who conceived you in love, working behind the scenes, helps you out."[1]

"... appearances don't impress me. I x-ray every motive and make sure you get what's coming to you."[2]

"You're blessed when you get your inside world—your mind and heart—put right. Then you can see God in the outside world."[3]

1.Matthew 6:1-4; 2.Revelation 2:23; 3.Matthew 5:8

"When you do something

for someone else,

don't call attention

to yourself."

Issue 33

The Stresses and Strains of life are Quietly Wearing me Down

"Here's what I want you to do: Find a quiet, secluded place so you won't be tempted to role-play before God. Just be there as simply and honestly as you can manage. The focus will shift from you to God, and you will begin to sense his grace."[1]

"Are you tired? Worn out? Burned out on religion? Come to me. Get away with me and you'll recover your life. I'll show you how to take a real rest. Walk with me and work with me—watch how I do it. Learn the unforced rhythms of grace. I won't lay anything heavy or ill-fitting on you. Keep company with me and you'll learn to live freely and lightly."[2]

... "Come off by yourselves; let's take a break and get a little rest." ...[3]

"... What I'm trying to do here is to get you to relax, to not be so preoccupied with *getting*, so you can respond to God's *giving*. People who don't know God and the way he works fuss over these things, but you know both God and how he works. Steep your life in God-reality, God-initiative, God-provisions. Don't worry about missing out. You'll find all your everyday human concerns will be met."[4]

1.Matthew 6:6; 2.Matthew 11:28-30; 3.Mark 6:31-32; 4.Matthew 6:31-34

"Keep company with me

and you'll learn

to live freely

and lightly."

Issue 34

What is Involved in Worshipping God?

"... the time is coming—it has, in fact, come—when what you're called will not matter and where you go to worship will not matter.

"It's who you are and the way you live that count before God. Your worship must engage your spirit in the pursuit of truth. That's the kind of people the Father is out looking for: those who are simply and honestly *themselves* before him in their worship. God is sheer being itself—Spirit. Those who worship him must do it out of their very being, their spirits, their true selves, in adoration."[1]

1 John 4:23-24

"Your worship **must**

engage *your spirit*

in the pursuit of truth."

Issue 35

How do I Become a True Disciple?

... "Anyone who comes to me but refuses to let go of father, mother, spouse, children, brothers, sisters—yes, even one's own self!—can't be my disciple. Anyone who won't shoulder his own cross and follow behind me can't be my disciple.

"Is there anyone here who, planning to build a new house, doesn't first sit down and figure the cost so you'll know if you can complete it? If you only get the foundation laid and then run out of money, you're going to look pretty foolish. Everyone passing by will poke fun at you: 'He started something he couldn't finish.'

"Or can you imagine a king going into battle against another king without first deciding whether it is possible with his ten thousand troops to face the twenty thousand troops of the other? And if he decides he can't, won't he send an emissary and work out a truce?

"Simply put, if you're not willing to take what is dearest to you, whether plans or people, and kiss it goodbye, you can't be my disciple."[1]

1. *Luke 14:26-33*

"Anyone who won't shoulder **his own cross** *and follow behind me can't be my disciple."*

Issue 36

How Concerned Should I Be About Social Issues?

"When he finally arrives, blazing in beauty and all his angels with him, the Son of Man will take his place on his glorious throne. Then all the nations will be arranged before him and he will sort the people out, much as a shepherd sorts out sheep and goats, putting sheep to his right and goats to his left.

"Then the King will say to those on his right, 'Enter, you who are blessed by my Father! Take what's coming to you in this kingdom. It's been ready for you since the world's foundation. And here's why:

I was hungry and you fed me,
I was thirsty and you gave me a drink,
I was homeless and you gave me a room,
I was shivering and you gave me clothes,
I was sick and you stopped to visit,
I was in prison and you came to me.'

"Then those 'sheep' are going to say, 'Master, what are you talking about? When did we ever see you hungry and feed you, thirsty and give you a drink? And when did we ever see you sick or in prison and come to you?' Then the King will say, 'I'm telling the solemn truth: Whenever you did one of these things to someone overlooked or ignored, that was me—you did it to me.'

"Then he will turn to the 'goats,' the ones on his left, and say, 'Get out, worthless goats! You're good for nothing but the fires of hell. And why? Because—

> I was hungry and you gave me no meal,
> I was thirsty and you gave me no drink,
> I was homeless and you gave me no bed,
> I was shivering and you gave me no clothes,
> Sick and in prison, and you never visited.'

"Then those 'goats' are going to say, 'Master, what are you talking about? When did we ever see you hungry or thirsty or homeless or shivering or sick or in prison and didn't help?'

"He will answer them, 'I'm telling the solemn truth: Whenever you failed to do one of these things to someone who was being overlooked or ignored, that was me—you failed to do it to me.'"[1]

1.Matthew 25:34-45

"Whenever you did one of these things to someone overlooked or ignored, that was me— you did it to me."

Issue 37

Where I Work it's Hard Being a Christian

"If you find the godless world is hating you, remember it got its start hating me. If you lived on the world's terms, the world would love you as one of its own. But since I picked you to live on God's terms and no longer on the world's terms, the world is going to hate you.

"When that happens, remember this: Servants don't get better treatment than their masters. If they beat on me, they will certainly beat on you. ..."[1]

"Don't be bluffed into silence by the treats of bullies. There's nothing they can do to your soul, your core being. Save your fear for God, who holds your entire life—body and soul—in his hands."[2]

"Count yourself blessed every time someone cuts you down or throws you out, every time someone smears or blackens your name to discredit me. What it means is that the truth is too close for comfort and that that person is uncomfortable. You can be glad when that happens—skip like a lamb, if you like!—for even though they don't like it, I do . . . and all heaven applauds. And know that you are in good company; my preachers and witnesses have always been treated like this."[3]

1.John 15:19-21; 2.Matthew 10:28; 3.Luke 6:22-23

"And know that you are in good company; my preachers and witnesses have always been treated like this."

Issue 38

My problem is I find it Easier to Compromise than to Stand out Against the Crowd

"Let me tell you why you are here. You're here to be salt-seasoning that brings out the God-flavors of this earth. If you lose your saltiness, how will people taste godliness? You've lost your usefulness and will end up in the garbage.

"Here's another way to put it: You're here to be light, bringing out the God-colours in the world. God is not a secret to be kept. We're going public with this, as public as a city on a hill. If I make you light-bearers, you don't think I'm going to hide you under a bucket, do you? I'm putting you on a light stand. Now that I've put you there on a hilltop, on a light stand—shine! Keep open house; be generous with your lives. By opening up to others, you'll prompt people to open up with God, this generous Father in heaven."[1]

"Stand up for me against world opinion and I'll stand up for you before my Father in heaven. If you turn tail and run, do you think I'll cover for you?"[2]

1.Matthew 5:13-16; 2.Matthew 10:32-33

"If you lose

your saltiness,

how will people taste

godliness?"

Issue 39

HOW am I to view the Many non-Christian Religions that are in The World?

"Let me set this before you as plainly as I can. If a person climbs over or through the fence of a sheep pen instead of going through the gate, you know he's up to no good—a sheep rustler! The shepherd walks right up to the gate. The gatekeeper opens the gate to him and the sheep recognize his voice. He calls his own sheep by name and leads them out. When he gets them all out, he leads them and they follow because they are familiar with his voice. They won't follow a stranger's voice but will scatter because they aren't used to the sound of it."

... "I'll be explicit ... I am the Gate for the sheep. All those others are up to no good—sheep stealers, every one of them. But the sheep didn't listen to them. I am the Gate. Anyone who goes through me will be cared for—will freely go in and out, and find pasture. ..."[1]

... "I am the Road, also the Truth, also the Life. No one gets to the Father apart from me. ..."[2]

1.John 10:1-9; 2.John 14:6

"I am the Gate for the sheep.

All those others are up to no good—

sheep stealers,

every one of them."

Issue 40

What is the PATH To GREATNESS in Your Kingdom?

"... You become great by accepting, not asserting. Your spirit, not your size, makes the difference."[1]

"... A servant is not ranked above his master; an employee doesn't give orders to the employer. If you understand what I'm telling you, act like it—and live a blessed life."[2]

"... And don't let people maneuver you into taking charge of them. There is only one Life-Leader for you and them—Christ.

"Do you want to stand out? Then step down. Be a servant. If you puff yourself up, you'll get the wind knocked out of you. But if you're content to simply be yourself, your life will count for plenty."[3]

1.Luke 9:46-48; 2.John 13:16-17; 3.Matthew 23:10-12

"Your spirit,

not your size,

makes the difference."

Issue 41

Is Marriage for Everyone?

... "Not everyone is mature enough to live a married life. It requires a certain aptitude and grace. Marriage isn't for everyone. Some, from birth seemingly, never give marriage a thought. Others never get asked—or accepted. And some decide not to get married for kingdom reasons. But if you're capable of growing into the largeness of marriage, do it."[1]

1.Matthew 19:11-12

"Marriage isn't *for everyone."*

ISSUE 42

WHAT ABOUT DIVORCE?

... "Haven't you read in your Bible that the Creator originally made man and woman for each other, male and female? And because of this, a man leaves father and mother and is firmly bonded to his wife, becoming one flesh—no longer two bodies but one. Because God created this organic union of the two sexes, no one should desecrate his art by cutting them apart...

... "Moses provided for divorce as a concession to your hardheartedness, but it is not part of God's original plan. I'm holding you to the original plan, and holding you liable for adultery if you divorce your faithful wife and then marry someone else. I make an exception in cases where the spouse has committed adultery."[1]

"Remember the Scripture that says, 'Whoever divorces his wife, let him do it legally, giving her divorce papers and her legal rights'? Too many of you are using that as a cover for selfishness and whim, pretending to be righteous just because you are 'legal.' Please, no more pretending. If you divorce your wife, you're responsible for making her an adulteress (unless she has already made herself that by sexual promiscuity). And if you marry such a divorced adulteress, you're automatically an adulterer yourself. You can't use legal cover to mask a moral failure."[2]

1.Matthew 19:4-9; 2.Matthew 5:31-32

"You can't use legal cover **to mask** *a moral failure."*

Issue 43

How do I get more faith?

"You don't need *more* faith. There is no 'more' or 'less' in faith. If you have a bare kernel of faith, say the size of a poppy seed, you could say to this sycamore tree, 'Go jump in the lake,' and it would do it."[1]

... "Embrace this God-life. Really embrace it, and nothing will be too much for you. This mountain, for instance: Just say, 'Go jump in the lake'—no shuffling or shilly-shallying—and it's as good as done. That's why I urge you to pray for absolutely everything, ranging from small to large. Include everything as you embrace this God-life, and you'll get God's everything. And when you assume the posture of prayer, remember that it's not all *asking*. If you have anything against someone, *forgive*—only then will your heavenly Father be inclined to also wipe your slate clean of sins."[2]

"... Don't you believe that I am in the Father and the Father is in me? The words that I speak to you aren't mere words. I don't just make them up on my own. The Father who resides in me crafts each word into a divine act.

"Believe me: I am in my Father and my Father is in me. If you can't believe that, believe what you see—these works. The person who trusts me will not only do what I'm doing but even greater things, because I, on my way to the Father, am giving you the same work to do that I've been doing. You can count on it. From now on, whatever you request along the lines of who I am and what I am doing, I'll do it. That's how the Father will be seen for who he is in the Son. I mean it. Whatever you request in this way, I'll do."[3]

1.Luke 17:6; 2.Mark 11:22-25; 3.John 14:10-14

"Embrace this God-life.

Really embrace it,

and nothing will be

too much for you."

Issue 44

I am not Tired Of Your service, but I am Tired In it

"Here's what I want you to do: Find a quiet, secluded place so you won't be tempted to role-play before God. Just be there as simply and honestly as you can manage. The focus will shift from you to God, and you will begin to sense his grace."[1]

"Are you tired? Worn out? Burned out on religion? Come to me. Get away with me and you'll recover your life. I'll show you how to take a real rest. Walk with me and work with me—watch how I do it. Learn the unforced rhythms of grace. I won't lay anything heavy or ill-fitting on you. ..."[2]

"My grace is enough; it's all you need.
My strength comes into its own in your weakness."[3]

1.Matthew 6:6; 2.Matthew 11:28-29; 3.2 Corinthians 12:9

"Learn the

unforced rhythms

of grace."

Issue 45

What should be My Attitude to those who Persecute me for being a Christian?

"… Here's what I propose: 'Don't hit back at all.' If someone strikes you, stand there and take it. If someone drags you into court and sues for the shirt off your back, giftwrap your best coat and make a present of it. And if someone takes unfair advantage of you, use the occasion to practice the servant life. No more tit-for-tat stuff. Live generously.

"You're familiar with the old written law, 'Love your friend,' and its unwritten companion, 'Hate your enemy.' I'm challenging that. I'm telling you to love your enemies. Let them bring out the best in you, not the worst. When someone gives you a hard time, respond with the energies of prayer, for then you are working out of your true selves, your God-created selves. This is what God does. He gives his best—the sun to warm and the rain to nourish—to everyone, regardless: the good and bad, the nice and nasty. If all you do is love the lovable, do you expect a bonus? Anybody can do that. If you simply say hello to those who greet you, do you expect a medal? Any run-of-the-mill sinner does that.

"In a word, what I'm saying is, *Grow up*. You're kingdom subjects. Now live like it. Live out your God-created identity. Live generously and graciously toward others, the way God lives toward you."[1]

"... Our Father is kind; you be kind. "[2]

1.Matthew 5:38-48; 2.Luke 6:36

"... love your enemies.

Let them bring out

the best in you,

not the worst."

Issue 46

How Long Must I Go On Forgiving?

"… Try seventy times seven.

"The kingdom of God is like a king who decided to square accounts with his servants. As he got under way, one servant was brought before him who had run up a debt of a hundred thousand dollars. He couldn't pay up, so the king ordered the man, along with his wife, children, and goods, to be auctioned off at the slave market.

"The poor wretch threw himself at the king's feet and begged, 'Give me a chance and I'll pay it all back.' Touched by his plea, the king let him off, erasing the debt.

"The servant was no sooner out of the room when he came upon one of his fellow servants who owed him ten dollars. He seized him by the throat and demanded, 'Pay up. Now!'

"The poor wretch threw himself down and begged, 'Give me a chance and I'll pay it all back.' But he wouldn't do it. He had him arrested and put in jail until the debt was paid. When the other servants saw this going on, they were outraged and brought a detailed report to the king.

"The king summoned the man and said, 'You evil servant! I forgave your entire debt when you begged me for mercy. Shouldn't you be compelled to be merciful to your fellow servant who asked for mercy?' The king was furious and put the screws to the man until he paid back his entire debt. And that's exactly what my Father in heaven is going to do to each one of you who doesn't forgive unconditionally anyone who asks for mercy."[1]

1.Matthew 18:21-35

"*Try* *seventy times seven.*"

Issue 47

There are Times when I Feel Uncertain about God's Love for Me

"This is how much God loved the world: He gave his Son, his one and only Son. And this is why: so that no one need be destroyed; by believing in him, anyone can have a whole and lasting life. God didn't go to all the trouble of sending his Son merely to point an accusing finger, telling the world how bad it was. He came to help, to put the world right again. ..."[1]

"... Because you've gone out on a limb, committed yourselves to love and trust in me, believing I came directly from the Father, the Father loves you directly. ..."[2]

1.John 3:16-17; 2.John 16:27

"This is how much

God loved the world:

He gave his Son,

his one and only Son."

Issue 48

My WORK is so DEMANDING it leaves Little Time for SPIRITUAL DEVELOPMENT

"... Take care! Protect yourself against the least bit of greed. Life is not defined by what you have, even when you have a lot."

... "The farm of a certain rich man produced a terrific crop. He talked to himself: 'What can I do? My barn isn't big enough for this harvest.' Then he said, 'Here's what I'll do: I'll tear down my barns and build bigger ones. Then I'll gather in all my grain and goods, and I'll say to myself, "Self, you've done well! You've got it made and can now retire. Take it easy and have the time of your life!" '

"Just then God showed up and said, 'Fool! Tonight you die. And your barnful of goods—who gets it?'

"That's what happens when you fill your barn with Self and not with God."[1]

"But be on your guard. Don't let the sharp edge of your expectation get dulled by parties and drinking and shopping. Otherwise, that Day is going to take you by complete surprise, spring on you suddenly like a trap, for it's going to come on everyone, everywhere, at once. ..."[2]

"And the seed that fell in the weeds—well, these are the ones who hear, but then the seed is crowded out and nothing comes of it as they go about their lives worrying about tomorrow, making money and having fun."[3]

1.Luke 12:15-21; 2.Luke 21:34-35; 3.Luke 8:14

"Life is not defined by what you have, even when you have a lot."

Issue 49

I Have Given Up so much to be a Christian. I Sometimes wonder if it's Worth It

... "Mark my words, no one who sacrifices house, brothers, sisters, mother, father, children, land—whatever—because of me and the Message will lose out. They'll get it all back, but multiplied many times in homes, brothers, sisters, mothers, children and land—but also in troubles. And then the bonus of eternal life! This is once again the Great Reversal: Many who are first will end up last, and the last first."[1]

"... And you've stuck with me through thick and thin. Now I confer on you the royal authority my Father conferred on me so you can eat and drink at my table in my kingdom and be strengthened as you take up responsibilities among the congregations of God's people."[2]

1.Mark 10.29-31; 2.Luke 22:28-30

"And you've stuck with me through thick and thin. Now I confer on you the royal authority my Father conferred on me ..."

Issue 50

Since I became a Christian my friends and family don't seem to understand me

"When people realize it is the living God you are presenting and not some idol that makes them feel good, they are going to turn on you, even people in your own family. There is a great irony here: proclaiming so much love, experiencing so much hate! But don't quit. Don't cave in. It is all well worth it in the end."[1]

"Don't be naive. Some people will impugn your motives, others will smear your reputation—just because you believe in me. Don't be upset when they haul you before the civil authorities. Without knowing it, they've done you—and me—a favor, given you a platform for preaching the kingdom news! And don't worry about what you'll say or how you'll say it. The right words will be there; the Spirit of your Father will supply the words."[2]

"Stay alert. This is hazardous work I'm assigning you. You're going to be like sheep running through a wolf pack, so don't call attention to yourselves. Be as cunning as a snake, inoffensive as a dove."[3]

"If you find the godless world is hating you, remember it got its start hating me. If you lived on the world's terms, the world would love you as one of its own. But since I picked you to live on God's terms and no longer on the world's terms, the world is going to hate you.

"When that happens, remember this: Servants don't get better treatment than their masters. If they beat on me, they will certainly beat on you. If they did what I told them, they will do what you tell them.

"They are going to do all these things to you because of the way they treated me, because they don't know the One who sent me. ..."[4]

"I've told you these things to prepare you for rough times ahead. They are going to throw you out of the meeting places. There will even come a time when anyone who kills you will think he's doing God a favor. They will do these things because they never really understood the Father. I've told you these things so that when the time comes and they start in on you, you'll be well-warned and ready for them."[5]

1.Matthew 10:21-22; 2.Matthew 10:17-20; 3.Matthew 10:16;

4.John 15:18-21; 5.John 16:1-4

*"But **don't quit.***

Don't cave in.

It is all well worth it

in the end."

NATIONAL DISTRIBUTORS

UK (and countries not listed below): CWR, PO Box 230, Farnham, Surrey GU9 8XG. Tel: 01252 784710 Outside UK (44) 1252 784710

AUSTRALIA: CMC Australasia, PO Box 519, Belmont, Victoria 3216. Tel: (03) 5241 3288

CANADA: CMC Distribution Ltd., PO Box 7000, Niagara on the Lake, Ontario L0S 1J0. Tel: 1 800 325 1297

GHANA: Challenge Enterprises of Ghana, PO Box 5723, Accra. Tel: (21) 222437 / 223249 Fax: 226227

INDIA: Crystal Communications, Plot No. 83, Sesachalla Society, Entrenchment Road, East Marredpalli, Secunderabad, Andhra Pradesh 500 026. Tel: (40) 7732511 / 7730577

KENYA: Keswick Bookshop, PO Box 10242, Nairobi. Tel: (02) 331692/226047

MALAYSIA: Salvation Book Centre (M) Sdn. Bhd., 23 Jalan SS 2/4, 47300 Petaling Jaya, Selangor. Tel: (603) 78766411 / 78766797 Fax: (603) 78757066

NEW ZEALAND: CMC New Zealand Ltd., Private Bag, 17910 Green Lane, Auckland. Tel: 09 5249393 Fax: 09 5222137

NIGERIA:FBFM, (Every Day with Jesus), Prince's Court, 37 Ahmed Onibudo Street, PO Box 70952, Victoria Island. Tel: 01 2617721, 616832, 4700218, 2619156

PHILIPPINES: Praise Incorporated, 145 Panay Avenue, Cor Sgt Esguerra St, Quezon City. Tel: 632 920 5291 Fax: 920 5747

REPUBLIC OF IRELAND: Scripture Union, 40 Talbot Street, Dublin 1. Tel: (01) 8363764

SINGAPORE:Campus Crusade Asia Ltd., 315 Outram Road, 06–08 Tan Boon Liat Building, Singapore 169074. Tel: (65) 222 3640

SOUTH AFRICA: Struik Christian Books (Pty Ltd), PO Box 193, Maitland 7405, Cape Town. Tel: (021) 551 5900

SRI LANKA: Christombu Books, 27 Hospital Street, Colombo 1. Tel: (1) 433142/328909

TANZANIA: City Christian Bookshop, PO Box 33463, Dar es Salaam. Tel: (51) 28915

UGANDA: New Day Bookshop, PO Box 2021, Kampala. Tel: (41) 255377

USA: CMC Distribution, PO Box 644, Lewiston, New York 14092-0644. Tel: 1 800 325 1297

ZIMBABWE: Word of Life Books, Shop 4, Memorial Bldg., 32 S Machel Ave., Harare. Tel: 781305 Fax: 774739

A FRESH VISION OF GOD
(SOFTBACK BOOK)

The Vision of God, From Confusion to Confidence, The Beatitudes, The Power of a New Perspective, The Corn of Wheat Afraid to Die, Heaven-sent Revival.

ISBN 1 85345 121 5 376 pp

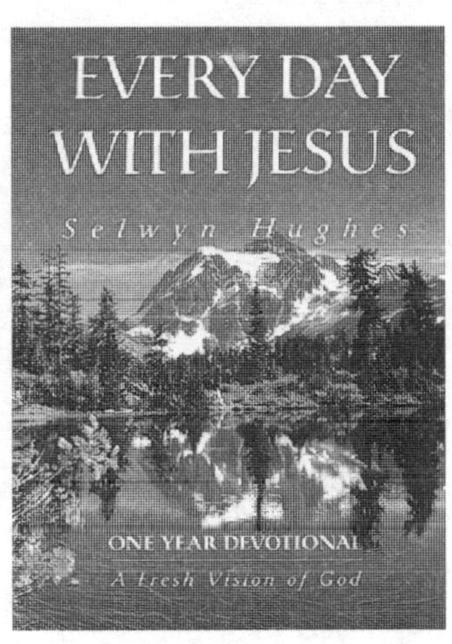

WATER FOR THE SOUL
(SOFTBACK BOOK)

Staying Spiritually Fresh, Rebuilding Broken Walls, The Character of God, When Sovereignty Surprises, The Fruit of the Spirit, Seven Pillars of Wisdom.

ISBN 1 85345 128 2 376 pp

Available from Christian bookshops or by post from National Distributors

Every Day Light

Light for the Path
(hardback book)

We've selected six of the best-loved editions of *Every Day with Jesus,* arranged them in undated order for a year of daily reading, and given them a touch of luxury to create three very special gift items – for yourself or others.

Every Day Light – Light for the Path features a complete commentary by Selwyn Hughes and additional further study sections on six topics:

* The Uniqueness of our Faith
* The Search for Meaning
* The Twenty-third Psalm
* The Spirit-filled Life
* Strong at the Broken Places
* Going Deeper with God

(same text as *Every Day with Jesus – Light for the Path – One Year Devotional Vol. 3*)

ISBN 0 805 42143 2
388 pp

Available from Christian bookshops or by post from National Distributors

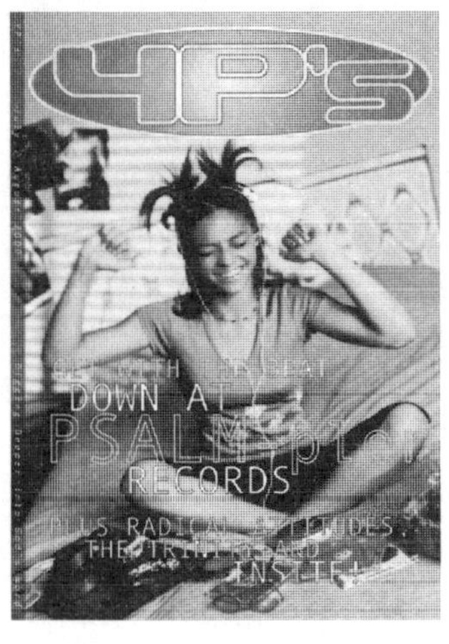

YP's (Young People's Every Day with Jesus)

YP's bi-monthly devotional for 12–16s with lively, contemporary graphics, interviews, humour, music reviews, competitions, special features and suggested prayers.

Topz (7–11-year -olds)

Topz bi-monthly devotional for 7–11s. The *Topz* gang teach children biblical truths reinforced by word games, puzzles, riddles, cartoons, competitions and simple prayers.

Available from Christian bookshops or by post from National Distributors

Every Day with Jesus for New Christians

"*Every Day with Jesus for New Christians* has become an important part of our discipleship programme and I highly recommend it to anyone looking for a powerful and relevant handbook for new Christians" – Gerald Coates.

YP's for New Christians

In just 30 days you can find out how completely mind-blowing life with God can be. Each day we try and explain how you can live your life for Jesus and start to get to grips with the Bible – His Word to us. So why not start today!

Topz for New Christians

Here's how to help 7–11-year-olds find faith in Jesus and have lots of fun exploring their new life with Him ... Day by day, *Topz for New Christians* Bible notes explain how we become God's friends, and how to grow closer to Jesus.

Available from Christian bookshops or by post from National Distributors

COVER TO COVER – THROUGH THE BIBLE AS IT HAPPENED (SOFTBACK BOOK)

Cover to Cover takes you on a time line through the Bible, following the events as they actually happened. Allow God to unfold His message to you over the year as you are guided through His Word. Featuring; a page-per-day reading plan, a 'bird's-eye view' of each Bible book, charts, maps, illustrations, diagrams and comments from Selwyn Hughes and Trevor Partridge which will assist you in drawing a personal challenge or encouragement from each day's reading.

ISBN 1 85345 136 3
448 pp

(same text as *Through the Bible*)

Available from Christian bookshops or by post from National Distributors